Original title:
That Awkward Moment When You Realize You're Alive

Copyright © 2025 Creative Arts Management OÜ
All rights reserved.

Author: Levi Montgomery
ISBN HARDBACK: 978-1-80566-035-4
ISBN PAPERBACK: 978-1-80566-330-0

When Time Takes a Breath

The clock ticked slow, like molasses on toast,
I tried to keep up, but I felt like a ghost.
Juggling life's lemons, I squirted my eye,
Laughter erupted, oh how I did cry!

Suddenly bright, the room started to spin,
A dance with my shadow, I'm laughing within.
Each tick became laughter, my thoughts took a leap,
With a wink at the cosmos, I embraced all the sheep.

Diving into the Depths of Now

Headfirst into chaos, I jumped with a grin,
Thoughts like a whirlpool, where do I begin?
Drowning in color, I swam with delight,
Mermaids of memory, they sparkled so bright.

Bubbling with giggles, I twirled and I swayed,
Every awkward glance was a fun little charade.
Waves of the present, they crashed at my feet,
Belly-flops of laughter made everything sweet.

The Strangeness of Familiar Places

Walking through alleys where I've never been,
Faces familiar, yet absent of skin.
Each brick held a secret, each corner a mime,
I chuckled at shadows that danced out of time.

Familiar yet funny, the world's out of place,
A slip on a banana, I'm losing my grace.
Eureka! I stumbled, oh what a delight,
Life's a big circus, and I'm in the spotlight.

The Nerve of Awareness

A tickle of thought, a spark of the brain,
With every new thought, I felt both delight and pain.
Awareness arrives, like a cat on the prowl,
Pouncing on wisdom, it made me how to howl.

I tiptoe through moments, cautious and bold,
Scared of the echoes my thoughts might unfold.
Yet laughter, my weapon, it never runs dry,
With each silly notion, I learned how to fly.

When the World Takes a Breath

I tripped on thin air, feeling so grand,
My coffee's still hot, but I've lost my plan.
Dancing with shadows, I missed my cue,
The cat just laughed; he knows what I knew.

Clouds gather high like a silly parade,
Laughter erupts, but it's a charade.
The sun took a break, then peeked through a tree,
Said, "Look at me shine; now you're just free!"

Mirages of Consciousness

My socks are mismatched, what a bold style,
I smile at the mirror, it questions my smile.
Thoughts run like rabbits, all racing my brain,
What's the prize again? Is it joy or just pain?

Pigeons convene and plot on the ledge,
I nod in agreement, then dance on the edge.
The world spins around, I find my left shoe,
Oh, it's all just a dream—wait, who's dreaming who?

The Pulse of Now

Life's like a sitcom, full of surprise,
I laugh so hard, I almost cry.
The clock is a jester, performing its tricks,
Each second a punchline, and I get the kicks.

Waking up feels like a game of charades,
Where I'm lost in a crowd of colorful shades.
The pizza guy chuckles, 'You ordered too late,'
I give him a wink, set the world straight!

When Reality Winks

Reality winks, and I fall off my chair,
Caught in a moment, I'm gasping for air.
The dog thinks I'm mad, my laugh like a bell,
Singing to the flowers, they know me too well.

A butterfly flutters, as if on a dare,
It joins in my jig; we dance in the air.
Life's a grand circus, each day is a show,
And I'm just the clown with a heart all aglow.

Revelations in Quietude

In a coffee shop, I sat to think,
The barista asked, 'Do you need a drink?'
I said, 'No thanks, just pondering life,'
As milk spilled, chaos, my thoughts caused strife.

A pigeon crapped on my newspaper page,
I laughed aloud, 'What a comical stage!'
Life's little mishaps, they dance and twirl,
In moments of stillness, they unfurl.

The Paradox of Being

Who knew the cat could judge so deep?
As I scrolled through memes, he fell asleep.
I thought, 'Asleep? Or in some wise trance?'
While I'm here worrying if I'll miss my chance.

The toaster burned while I pondered fate,
It popped my bread, said, 'It's never too late.'
Living's like dance, with two left feet,
Stumbling gracefully—sometimes not so neat.

Whispers of the Living

Under the stars, I tried to focus,
On life's meaning, amidst all the hocus.
A squirrel waved, or was that my mind?
In nature's chaos, clarity I'd find.

I spotted a raccoon, sass in his stride,
He stole my sandwich, with no shame or pride.
Life's absurdity, my new best friend,
In laughter, I see where the moments blend.

Shadows of Self-Discovery

In mirrors, shadows, I caught my gaze,
A perplexed face lost in the maze.
Do I smile? Or just look confused?
In this quest for self, I feel bemused.

Coffee stains mapped my day's long quest,
Turns out humor's my very best vest.
Between quirks and blunders, sweet life bursts,
In the awkwardness, my soul it thirsts.

Glimmering Threads of Reality

A sneeze in the silent room,
A moment of pure, wild glee.
Did I just spark a meme?
Reality giggles back at me.

Cats plotting world domination,
With eyes like tiny spies.
I ponder my contribution,
To breakfast's burnt surprise.

The clock ticks, a ticking foe,
Yet I'm glued to the TV.
Are those tacos in the show?
Or just my brain's big spree?

In the mirror, a face looks back,
We both seem quite bemused.
Is this the life I lack?
Am I enthusiastically confused?

Awakening to the Ordinary

Coffee spills like a wild stream,
Oh, what a glorious start!
Is this a nightmare dream?
Or just my morning art?

Birds chirp with a sing-song tune,
While I'm stuck in my pajamas.
Is that a dog or raccoon?
Life's a series of dramas.

My socks still don't match today,
Should I call it a fashion?
Disarray's my unique play,
In moments of pure passion.

Yet here I stand, bewildered,
In a world that seems too bright.
While I feel quite tethered,
To this chaotic delight.

Awkward Awakening

The alarm shrieked, I took a tumble,
   Into an outfit unplanned.
Why does Monday always grumble?
   With coffee I try to stand.

The toast pops like a cannon blast,
   My cat chases the crumbs.
Life's randomness unsurpassed,
   In a rhythm that just hums.

Slippers on the wrong feet,
   Each step feels like a dance.
Do my neighbors think I'm sweet,
   Or just give a sideways glance?

Yet here I am, bewildered mind,
   Laughing at my own parade.
In this life, joy I find,
   Even in the mess I made.

The Breath Between Thoughts

I pause, the world a spinning blur,
Did I really just trip so hard?
I could've sworn the ground was pure,
Yet here I stand, backyard bard.

Birds gossip like nature's news,
While I chase my own tail,
Today feels like a quirky fuse,
With adventure on a rail.

Peanut butter on my shoe,
Is that a fashion trend?
Do I start a new zoo?
Or just wait for this to end?

Yet here I stand, silly grin,
In this odd life's embrace.
Realizing I'm tucked within,
A joyful, goofy place.

The Shock of Being

One day I woke up in a jam,
Spilled my coffee on the cat, oh fam!
Forgot the toast and lost my shoe,
Is this what living really means? Who knew?

I tripped on the mat and hit the wall,
The silent house gave me a call.
I waved to my plants, they waved back slow,
Life is a circus, with a side of woe.

I found my keys inside the fridge,
And thought maybe I found a new bridge.
With socks that rarely match my style,
Each day I laugh, it's just my guile.

Each moment slips through like sand in the breeze,
I stop and ponder, say, "What's the tease?"
Why does the world spin all around?
Maybe it's just because I'm still here, unbound!

Echoes of a Heartbeat

In a world where time does flip,
And my brain takes its own little trip.
I hear my heart go thumpity-thump,
Who knew it had such a rhythmic pump?

I stood in the shower, shampoo in hand,
And forgot the lyrics to my rock band.
Singing loud, the neighbors glare,
But hey, it's my concert—do I care?

The cats were judging from their perch,
I told them life's a crazy search.
With every heartbeat, a new surprise,
Could they feel it too? All those sighs?

Moments of joy, wrapped tight like a hug,
I dance with my thoughts, give them a tug.
As I trip on my dreams, oh what a thrill,
Each echo whispers, yes, life is a drill!

Reflections in a Cracked Mirror

I gazed in the glass, what a sight I found,
Hair a wild nest, I'm fashion-bound!
The toothpaste smudged across my cheek,
Reflections chuckle, laughter's peak.

Every wrinkle tells a story true,
About mornings lost in my coffee brew.
In this cracked glass, I see my face,
An artist's palette, a mismatched grace.

Tried to look cool, gave a strut,
Tripped on my own foot, but what a nut!
These glimpses of me, a bit bizarre,
I'm living my truth, fantastic star!

With every glance, the humor grows,
Life's a sketch, full of highs and lows.
I smile at my flaws, embrace the cheer,
Through this cracked mirror, I see it clear!

A Dance of Consciousness

Two left feet in a tango spree,
Shuffling awkward, just let me be!
I step on toes, but giggles climb,
Life's a dance, with no set rhyme.

Each fleeting thought's a wobble and twirl,
My mind's a carnival, giving a whirl.
I dip and dive, emotions sway,
With each misstep, I laugh all day.

A pirouette into a cereal box,
Juggling breakfast, what a paradox!
The milk spills out, it's a slippery fate,
But who knew chaos could be so great?

In this dance of thoughts, I lose my way,
Yet somehow find joy in disarray.
With every turn, I learn to cope,
In this silly ballet, I find my hope!

Moments Between Heartbeats

In the stillness, I feel a twitch,
A sneeze, a laugh, a little hitch.
Life's hiccups joke, they poke and prod,
As if to say, 'Hey, you're not a god.'

I spill my drink, the world does spin,
A dance of chaos, let the games begin.
Trip on a sock, I tumble down,
The floor wears my face—my new crown.

A cat strolls past, so full of pride,
As if to say, 'There's no need to hide.'
I watch it strut, with a mighty flair,
While I'm just here, with food in my hair.

Chasing my thoughts, they run and flee,
Like butterflies trapped inside of me.
In every mishap, laughter's pure gold,
Life's wild antics—a joy to behold!

The Canvas of Existence

Brushstrokes of silence, a tickle of fate,
Colors collide, it's never too late.
With each splash of joy, and splatter of pain,
I'm painting my day in a quirky way.

A pigeon coos, it seems to conspire,
With crumbs around, I aim to inquire.
It struts and flaps, then it poops, oh dear,
A masterpiece ruined—let's grab a beer.

The sunbeams dance, they twirl and tease,
While bees buzz around, doing as they please.
I trip on my thoughts, knock over my cup,
This art of existence, 'Hey, what's up?'

Surrounded by laughter, quirky and bright,
I find myself laughing—what a sight!
The canvas is messy, but isn't that grand?
In a world so absurd, I take my stand!

Reflections at Dawn

Mirror, mirror, on the wall,
Why do I look like I just took a fall?
My hair's a mess, my eyes still glazed,
But hey, I'm here—life's quirky maze.

Birds start to chirp, a cacophony loud,
They sing of adventures, while I'm still cowed.
A sock on the floor, glaring at me,
This is my morning—such a spree!

Coffee brews, like magic it steams,
Awakens my senses, ignites my dreams.
A splash of milk, or is it my fate?
Every sip's louder—can't contemplate!

Outside, the world laughs, running amok,
While I'm just here, feeling like a duck.
Paddling through puddles of clumsy delight,
I stumble awake—what a beautiful sight!

Stirring from the Dream

From slumber I rise, feeling like goo,
Brain's still in dreams, what is my cue?
The clock ticks louder, a drum in my head,
As I contemplate breakfast, and diving in bed.

I juggle my socks, one red and one green,
Who knew fashion could be this obscene?
With toast in my teeth and a grin on my face,
I manage my morning with awkward grace.

Outside, the world hums a strange tune,
Squirrels are plotting, under the moon.
A jogger can't run without tripping on air,
Life's silly chaos floats everywhere!

Giggling at moments as they come and go,
In this weird little play, I steal the show.
With laughter, I dance on absurdity's road,
All hail the silly—my heart's lightened load!

The Undercurrents of Life

Woke up today, can't find my shoe,
Tripped on my cat, who knew it too.
Coffee spills, a morning spree,
Laughing at gravity's twisted glee.

In this dance of fate's design,
Falling leaves, I'm out of line.
Socks mismatched, yet I still stride,
Life's a carnival, nowhere to hide.

Every hiccup, a comic scene,
Juggling dreams with a side of beans.
Who knew chaos could feel so spry,
With every trip, I touch the sky.

Embracing quirks, they bring delight,
In the circus of day and night.
So here I laugh, as life unfolds,
In the dance of joy, I'm brave and bold.

The Playfulness of Breathing

Caught a breath, it tickles me,
Like sneezing fairies, it's hard to see.
Each inhale is a comedy show,
Exhales release all the woes, you know.

Laughter bubbles in my chest,
While counting how many times I rest.
Chest goes up, belly goes wide,
It's a roller coaster, can't help but ride.

Air balloons float, whimsical and bright,
Who knew breathing could lead to flight?
With every gulp, more laughs arrive,
In the game of life, I cleverly thrive.

Chasing down every airy note,
With a giggle, I'll happily float.
In this play of breaths and sighs,
The fun is found in sweet surprise.

Chasing Shadows of Truth

Stumbling upon shadows in the park,
Like lost socks that miss their mark.
Truth winks slyly from behind a tree,
Saying, 'Catch me if you can, you see?'

I trip over thoughts, fractured and free,
Trying to chase what's not meant to be.
With every twist, I find myself lost,
But who counts the cost of wobbly thoughts?

Laughter hides where seriousness lurks,
In the puzzles life hands, filled with quirks.
Chasing shadows beneath the sun,
In this game of light, we're all just fun.

So let's play tag with the lies we weave,
Finding humor in what we believe.
In the chase, there's joy to gain,
Painting life's canvas with laughter's stain.

The Art of Being Uncomfortable

Sitting on benches that squeak and moan,
Where fidgeting legs feel like a drone.
Wriggling in fabric two sizes too tight,
Finding humor in this awkward plight.

Unruly hair in the gusty breeze,
Glimpsing reflections that tease and please.
I smile at mirrors that wobble and sway,
In the clumsy dance of everyday play.

Bumping into folks, saying 'Oops, my bad!',
In the crowd of life, it's not always rad.
But laughter's the glue that keeps it intact,
In this maze of mishaps, joy's not lacked.

So embrace the weird, the twist, the turn,
With every fumble, I start to learn.
In the art of being wildly unsure,
It's the playful heart that keeps us pure.

Flickering Lights of Recognition

Stumbling through the noise of life,
Tripping on the edge of strife.
My coffee spills, my socks don't match,
But hey, I'm here, let's have a catch.

A bird steals fries from my plate,
It squawks and flaps, oh how irate!
I laugh so hard that I might snort,
In this grand circus, I'm full of sport.

The light flickers above my head,
Does someone know my thoughts unread?
I hit the switch, it chirps in glee,
Hello, world! You can't outrun me!

So here I dance, both wild and free,
With ketchup stains on my torn knee.
In this comedy of life's delight,
I find a smile in each silly sight.

Heartbeats and Hiccups

A little jump, a sudden glitch,
My heart's a drum, don't change the pitch!
The hiccup comes, I hold my breath,
What a way to mock sweet death!

I trip on air, my shoes untied,
The world laughs on, I just glide!
Each heartbeat hums a silly tune,
Can't help but dance beneath the moon.

I spill water on my lap, oh dear,
Let's make that a fountain of cheer!
Here's to the quirky, the small, the slight,
Life's a riddle, and we delight!

So let's embrace this wobbly ride,
With every jolt, let joy decide.
For in this chaos, we find our grace,
With laughter, we'll always keep pace.

Navigating the Maze of Being

Lost in a maze of socks and shoes,
Spinning around, I can't choose.
Which way to go? The left or right?
I'll just follow the twinkling light.

Funny signs point everywhere,
"Watch your step!" "Beware the stare!"
A cat walks by, judging my style,
I shrug and grin, can't stop my smile.

Through twists and turns, I find my way,
Each corner holds a brand new play.
A hamster wheel spins in my mind,
Wishing for snacks of all kinds!

But wait, I spot a mirror's gleam,
A stranger smiles, or is it a dream?
I wave hello, then wave goodbye,
In this maze, we're all just sly.

The Lightness of Being Unveiled

With feathers on my head, I waddle,
Strutting 'round like some huge model.
The sun peeks down, a cheeky grin,
Life's a show, and I'm in to win!

Balancing joy on a tightrope thin,
I toss out jokes, let the fun begin!
Each chuckle's a balloon, light and free,
Floating high, just like me!

The world spins 'round in colors bright,
I twirl and whirl, what a thrilling sight.
A tap dance here, a leap over there,
Oh laughter, you're the sweetest air!

So here's to lightness, to joyful zest,
In this crazy life, I feel so blessed.
I'll wear my quirks like a shiny badge,
In the grand parade, let's all be glad!

Footprints on Ephemeral Sands

Woke up today, forgot my shoes,
Did I leave my brain? It seems to snooze.
Sandy shores, my thoughts drift away,
Crabs judging me, they watch me play.

Seagulls squawk, a noisy choir,
Do they think my dance is dire?
Chasing waves, I slip and slide,
Nature giggles, it won't abide.

Footprints washed, my past erased,
Ocean waves, they seem quite rased.
Bathing in laughter, I soak it in,
Life's a joke, I'm just here for the spin.

With every splash, a new surprise,
Sandcastle dreams under sunny skies.
Who knew existence could be so fun?
I'll dance with the tide till the day is done.

The Dissonance of Living

Alarm goes off, it's time to rise,
Hitting snooze feels oh so wise.
Coffee spills, a morning show,
I'm not a pro, just a caffeine show.

Missed my train, oh what a sight,
Running late, I feel the fright.
Bouncing off walls, a chaotic dance,
Life's a game where I have no chance.

Strangers smile, or is it a glare?
I wave back, but do they care?
In this circus of daily grind,
The punchline is always hard to find.

Yet here I am, a jester's role,
Riding life's whims, that's my goal.
Laughter echoes in the fray,
Dissonance reigns, come what may.

Tangles in the Fabric of Time

Tick-tock goes the big old clock,
Lost my sock, but who's to mock?
Time's a loop, a funny twist,
I chase the minutes, can't resist.

Yesterday's lunch, stuck in my brain,
Are those leftovers? What's the gain?
Whirling thoughts, all intertwine,
In this maze, is it yours or mine?

Faded jeans, too tight at the seams,
Caught in this dance of silly dreams.
Each moment bends like silly clay,
In the fabric of time, I'll lose my way.

But here I twirl, and here I grin,
Life's a riddle where I begin.
Catching giggles, juggling the hours,
In this laugh, I find my powers.

A Kaleidoscope of Realization

Spinning 'round in a vibrant haze,
The world shifts colors in whimsical ways.
Whispers of joy in a jumbled kaleidoscope,
Life's a puzzle, lacking in hope.

Umbrellas turned wrong when skies pour down,
I wear my mistakes like a silly crown.
Every splash brings a chuckle and sigh,
Who knew the storm would make me fly?

Riding the waves of this clumsy fate,
Can't help but laugh, it's never too late.
Through the chaos, I spin and glide,
In this strange dance, I find my pride.

With every twist, a new hue shines,
Living's a painting with playful lines.
In the absurd, my heart takes flight,
A colorful journey through day and night.

Echoes of Awakening

Waking up to yesterday's sock,
Coffee spills, what a shocking shock.
Chasing dreams like a cat on a spree,
Wondering loudly, "Is this really me?"

Mirror says, "Hey, look at you!"
Hair's a nest, and that's nothing new.
A dance with chaos, a giggle in tow,
Life's odd rhythm is all I know.

Stumbling 'round like a newborn deer,
Tripping over thoughts, and things unclear.
Each moment's a plot twist, oh what fun,
Heart's laughing loudly, this race is won.

Tomorrow's worries? Let them all fly,
I'm busy figuring out how to tie.
A laugh, a smile, all in a row,
Being alive is the best kind of show!

Breath of the Unseen

In the fridge, leftovers dance with fate,
Pie from a week, but it looks quite great.
Oops, is that mold? Time for a feast—
Comedic kitchen, humor released.

Stepping outside, sun tickles the nose,
Do I really have shoes on? Who knows!
Chasing the bee that won't take a hint,
It's like I'm the jester, wearing a splint.

Laughter bubbles with each silly thought,
Awareness creeps in, a battle I fought.
Forget the to-do, let joy take the reign,
What's planned for today? Just a fun little game.

Whispers from trees, secrets to find,
Nature's a comedian, oh, it's so kind.
Breath of the unseen, a giggle or two,
Live in the moment? I might just do.

Sudden Awareness in Twilight

Twilight creeps with a wink and a grin,
Caught in a snap, where should I begin?
Stuffed in the couch like a potato chip,
Finding my focus on a chocolate dip.

Stars peep out, each one a spark,
My brain's like a firefly lost in the dark.
Thoughts like confetti, they scatter and swirl,
Reality's a prank, my mind's in a whirl.

Each giggle echoes, a sweet little tease,
Is life a joke or just warm summer breeze?
Chasing the dusk, my inner clown prances,
Lost in the laughter, oh, how it dances.

Living it large, with whimsy and flair,
Who knew awareness would bring such a scare?
A jest in the evening, with joy as my guide,
Sudden delight, I'm humor's best ride.

Dancing with the Present

Wobbling through life like a sailboat's drift,
Time skips a beat, it's a quirky gift.
With every misstep, laughter takes flight,
The dance of the moment, oh, what a sight!

Each glance in the mirror reveals a surprise,
Who's that goofball with wide-open eyes?
Confidence shakes with a side of cheese,
In this odd ballet, just do what you please.

A toe-tapping story in each clumsy spin,
Life's piñata bursts, let the fun begin!
Forget perfection, embrace all the quirks,
Each silly twirl is where joy really lurks.

So here's to the jive, and here's to the sway,
Every odd moment will entrance in its play.
Dancing with life on a floor of delight,
I'm waltzing with joy into the night.

From Silence to Clarity

In the stillness, thoughts can roam,
Like squirrels in a tree, they call it home.
Stumbling on ideas, tripping on grace,
Who knew this brain was such a wild place?

Coffee spills, and so do dreams,
Life's a jigsaw, bursting at the seams.
Pants on backward, shoes untied,
Laughing at the chaos, I cannot hide.

Clarity dances just out of reach,
Offering wisdom, like a strange peach.
A wiggle, a giggle, sometimes a shout,
Oh look, I'm alive, let's figure it out!

Jokes in my head, I can't catch the bus,
Reality fumbles, it's all a plus.
With each quirky turn, I cheerfully thrive,
In this carnival of thoughts, I must dive!

The Light Within Shadows

Shadows creep where light does play,
Twisting thoughts in a humorous way.
A chuckle hides in the gloom, it seems,
Who knew my life was full of memes?

Grinning at how the day unfolds,
Finding treasure in things untold.
In the corners, giggles arise,
With every mishap, a surprise!

Sunshine peeks through, a sales pitch bright,
"Buy two smiles; you'll get joy tonight!"
Thoughts flicker, but laughter is grand,
Turning all fumbles into something planned.

Amongst the silliness, a truth does gleam,
Shadows recede, revealing a dream.
Embrace the blunders, let laughter entwine,
For the light that we find, is foolishly divine!

The Taste of Living

Life's like a buffet laid out wide,
Sampling joy with a side of pride.
A sprinkle of mess, a dash of fun,
With every bite, I'm on the run!

Hot coffee spills, "Oops"—a morning thrill,
The croissant was singing, "You eat at will!"
Taste the laughter, chew on the zest,
In this feast of chaos, I'm truly blessed.

Crispy hiccups and zesty slips,
Waltzing through life, on crumbly trips.
Desserts of whimsy, snacks to share,
We're all just kids without a care.

So here's to flavors too wild to tame,
Eating life's stories, all in the game.
Take a big bite, don't fear the dive,
In this tasty adventure, I'm so alive!

Sips of Awareness

A sip of tea, a taste of zing,
Every brew shows how much I cling.
To moments that quirk, to laughter so bright,
Awareness brews in the soft twilight.

Cups overflow with giggles and glee,
Sipping on insights, oh can't you see?
The world's a comedy, a wonderful show,
Brewed in the chaos, with plenty to show.

With each clink of glass, a realization stirs,
Life's a party, with twirls and whirs.
Dancing with joy, I spill out my drink,
Forgotten the worries, let's wander and blink!

So here's to the sips, the spills, and the fun,
Awareness is brewing, we're all under one sun.
Let's raise our cups, toast to the ride,
In this whimsical journey, I'll take it all in stride!

The Faint Pulse of Truth

In the mirror, I glance and blink,
A double take, makes me think.
Was that a smile or just a grin?
Life's a circus, let the show begin.

Coffee spills on my favorite shirt,
I laugh it off, could be worse.
Why take life seriously, I plead?
A clumsy dance is all we need.

Juggling tasks but dropping balls,
Life's a game, or so it calls.
With each trip, I find my stride,
In this chaos, I take pride.

So here I am, with joy in hand,
Absurdity, my merry band.
Every stutter, every fall,
Makes this living thing a ball.

Whispers From the Void

Midnight snacks, crumbs in my bed,
A race with time, I'm always fed.
The fridge hums softly, an ally near,
Whispers from the void, loud and clear.

I trip on thoughts that float like dreams,
Falling into reality's seams.
Who lit the stars? Was it my cat?
His purring louder than any pat.

Conversations with socks left astray,
They never answer, but that's okay.
Life's a joke, I'm the punchline,
Trying to dance on a frayed line.

At each mishap, I raise a brow,
What's next in store? I'll make it wow.
So here I sit, with crumbs and cheer,
Laughing at the chaos, that much is clear.

Frayed Ends of Reality

Tangled thoughts, a messy thread,
Life it seems, is more like bread.
Toast it lightly, spread some jam,
Savoring bites like who I am.

Mistakes are just quirky charms,
Falling for grace, with open arms.
Life's a canvas, colors fly,
Painting giggles with every sigh.

Pillow fort meetings in the light,
Discussing dreams that take flight.
A cardboard kingdom, we all reign,
Making the mundane feel insane.

Laughing at shadows that stretch and twist,
Wondering why we even exist.
With joy I trudge through each day's end,
In this comic tale, I often bend.

The Humor of Existence

Dancing through puddles, splashes galore,
Every drop is a giggling roar.
Catching raindrops in open mouths,
Life's too silly, down south and north.

Emails mock me, a digital game,
We've become friends, yet feel the same.
Typing away in a caffeinated daze,
Celebrating blunders, in all their ways.

Each hiccup, a melody so sweet,
Stumbling on words, dancing on feet.
With every misstep, I proudly cheer,
Finding the humor, oh so near.

Laughter echoes in empty halls,
Inviting the absurd, where chaos calls.
So cheers to the moments, bright and strange,
In this wacky life, I'll never change.

Serendipity in Stillness

Sat on my couch, remote in hand,
Debating deep thoughts—can I understand?
The fridge hums tunes, a symphony plain,
While I ponder snacks and life's silly game.

A sock on the floor, a cat on my lap,
Both looking lost, perhaps in a nap.
Biscuit crumbs whisper tales of delight,
Who knew boredom could spark such insight?

My coffee's gone cold, yet I remain warm,
In a universe busily falling apart.
Each tick of the clock, a comedic charm,
Finding laughter in stillness—a true work of art.

Shouting at clouds, they just float on by,
As if mocking my small existential sigh.
The day rolls on, with giggles and cheer,
Serendipity thrives, let's raise a warm beer!

Laughing at Life's Ironies

Tripped on my laces, fell flat on my face,
Found the family dog, who joined in the race.
Each stumble a story, each slip a surprise,
Life seems a circus before my keen eyes.

The toaster burned toast, with a guilty grin,
Then laughed with the kettle, that chimed in its spin.
Bread confessions made me feel less alone,
As I crafted a sandwich, with humor now grown.

The cat gave me looks, both haughty and sly,
While up on the shelf sat a bowl of pie.
Life's grandest moments show just how we mix,
With irony served up, often leading to kicks.

So pass me the lemons, I'll make lemonade,
Where giggles and chuckles won't ever fade.
In this comedy script, we're all but absurd,
Take notice of joy in each silly word!

The Peculiar Thread of Consciousness

Awoke from a dream of epic cuisine,
Where tacos and dragons danced on the screen.
Thoughts thread and tangle, a curious maze,
Of deep revelations and bizarre essays.

Found my old diary, dusted with time,
Filled with crayons and rhymes that don't rhyme.
Each jotted down secret, a giggle in wait,
In this odd web of life, fate plays a great state.

Magic fish swam through calculations of rest,
As I pondered if onions were really the best.
With each bubble popped, I burst into glee,
Consciousness tickles, just like a bumblebee.

I chased fleeting thoughts, as they danced out of reach,
In the playground of wonder, they giggled and screeched.

Caught in their laughter, I throw back my head,
What a peculiar thread, this life that we've led!

Riddles Written in Air

Whispers float high, on a breeze so bizarre,
Questions like clouds, twinkling from afar.
Is that a banana, or just my own mind?
Riddles of life, in each moment I find.

Sipped tea on the porch, with no grand design,
While ants hold a meeting on tipsy old twine.
Life writes its riddles in melodies sweet,
All while I chuckle at how thoughts compete.

On a Wednesday morning, I tried to be wise,
Wore mismatched socks, a questionable guise.
And in the mirror, reflected my glee,
At the absurdity staring right back at me.

So let's toast the questions, raise cups to the play,
For riddles in air guide us through this ballet.
With laughter our compass, we will not despair,
Life's quirks and its riddles flow fresh through the air!

Nature's Gentle Nudge

A butterfly flutters by, it seems to wink,
I stop and ponder, then stare at my drink.
The world spins wild, like a carnival ride,
Reminding me gently, I'm here, and it's wide.

A squirrel steals crumbs from under my chair,
I think he knows something, a little affair.
He's living it up, with no cares in his mind,
While I sit and sip tea, feeling quite blind.

The trees start to giggle, their leaves in a sway,
They whisper of secrets, in breezy ballet.
I chuckle and wave, we're all in this dance,
Alive and a bit silly, at fate's wobbly chance.

Sunshine is grinning, it tickles my nose,
It's hard not to smile, as warmth gently glows.
With nature around, it's a wonderfully strange,
To experience life in its wild, funny range.

Shifting Shadows of Identity

In the mirror's reflection, a face I don't know,
I blink and I chuckle, is this the real show?
A mane of wild hair, like a tangled lost vine,
Who knew I would wake up a creature divine?

The clothes on my back seem to play hide and seek,
A mismatched parade that earns quite the cheek.
I spin in my room, like a dance on the floor,
Each twirl is a giggle, "What else is in store?"

The socks on my feet have a tale to unfold,
One polka dot, one stripe, breaking the mold.
Who says I can't blend in with a quirky flair?
Identity's funny, a riddle laid bare.

A voice in my head asks if I fit the vibe,
Grinning in silence as I choose to subscribe.
"Be you!" it insists, with a wink and a bow,
Life's a wild jest, let's just take a bow.

Breathing Life into Stillness

A cactus speaks softly, it sways in the breeze,
In its prickly wisdom, it brings me to ease.
It's quiet then loud, like a cat with a toy,
Stirring up laughter, it's all just a ploy.

On a cushion of clouds, I sit lost in thought,
Breathing deep with a hum, for calmness is sought.
Yet life springs a joke, a tickle in the air,
The stillness can giggle, "Oh, don't you dare!"

A rock rolls on by, with a chuckle it glints,
Is it me or the nature that plays with the hints?
I sit here and wonder, with glee in my heart,
Life's slapstick routine—a wild work of art!

As the sun winks down, I watch shadows play,
The stillness is vibrant in its own funny way.
So let's relish the pause, come laugh in the shade,
Breathe in the moments, let laughter cascade.

Unspoken Truths of the Present

A bird chirps a tune, then sings off-key,
Each note a reminder, just let it be free.
I look at my coffee, it spills like a mess,
Life's subtle remix, oh what a distress!

The clock on the wall seems to chuckle, then chime,
As seconds parade in their own silly rhyme.
I nod to the ticking, the rhythm so sly,
All of us dancing, just passing on by.

With each clumsy step on this up-and-down lane,
I trip on a word, then I giggle, not pain.
It's okay to be goofy, in love with the now,
An orchestra playing, a whimsical wow!

So raise up your glass, and toast to this jest,
The truth is we're living in life's crazy quest.
With laughter and joy, let's embark on the ride,
Unspoken but vivid, with me as your guide.

Colliding with the Present

I tripped on my thoughts, to my surprise,
A world sneezed loud, bright and alive!
The coffee spilled, oh sweet delight,
As I feasted on chaos in morning light.

Texting my feet to just sit still,
But phones claim wisdom with every thrill,
A squirrel stole my sandwich, proud and bold,
While I pondered snacks as treasures untold.

Reality rang like a curious bell,
As I shouted back, 'Can't you just tell?'
The shadows giggled, they seemed to play,
As I danced with the day in a clumsy sway.

Life's small moments, a gift on the run,
With laughter and blunders, here comes the fun,
So shine your quirks, let them be unchained,
For the wonders of living are cleverly gained.

Dancing with the Unnoticed

The dust bunnies waltz in the dusky light,
While I fumble and hope to get it right,
A sock's lost tango beneath the bed,
As thoughts pirouette inside my head.

The silent TV mocks my plight,
With news of the world buzzing bright,
I sip my thoughts like a fine, chilled brew,
Wondering if I'm just passing through.

A cat plays the piano with paws so spry,
While my lunch debates if it's meant to fly,
And pigeons exchange gossip on the street,
As I stumble and twirl on my two left feet.

In quirky moments, I find my space,
With chuckles and quirks defining my place,
For the unseen rhythm makes me feel grand,
In this dance of life, I'll take my stand.

Voices Beneath the Surface

Whispers of yesterday float on the breeze,
While thoughts weave and tumble like autumn leaves,
I chase polka-dots that fade on the run,
In a symphony of chaos, oh what fun!

The toaster burns bread, what a sight,
As ghosts in my kitchen argue with light,
I giggle at crumbs, my loyal friends,
In this funny world, where mischief never ends.

My shoes plot a trip to the fridge at night,
While the shadows hum tunes of pure delight,
With voices from corners, making me grin,
As I juggle my breakfast all over again.

In laughter's embrace, the oddness finds peace,
Among sparkles of life that never cease,
For the voices around me, a playful parade,
As I dance through the day in the glimmers we've made.

A Flicker of Understanding

Mirror's reflection wants me to smile,
But it fumbles and stumbles, just for a while,
A breakfast of crumbs on my cheek does reside,
As I ponder this journey, wide-eyed and tried.

The cat disapproves of my morning quest,
While I search for wisdom in mishaps unblessed,
In socks of mixed patterns, I stride without care,
And question if life's truly fair.

With coffee in hand, I salute the sun,
As birds chirp confessions about all their fun,
An odd gathering at the brunch of the day,
Showing me there's magic in the fray.

Through goofy mishaps and silly thoughts shared,
I dance with confusion, yet strangely prepared,
For the flicker of moments, peculiar yet bright,
In this circus of living, I find my delight.

The Jolt of Existence

A coffee spill in the morning light,
Awake I am, what a surprising sight!
Emails buzzing like busy bees,
Feeling alive with a hint of unease.

Jumped the wrong way at a shadow's play,
Is this reality or a comic display?
The toaster's pop, oh the thrill and the fright,
Who needs a horror when breakfast's a bite?

My knees crack like firewood in the breeze,
How can such sounds bring me to my knees?
Laughter bubbles up from nowhere near,
A happy dance, though the moves aren't clear.

Breath in, breath out, oh what a chore,
Life's a mix of comedy and folklore.
With every trip, stumble, and fall,
I'm grateful for this wonderfully weird call.

A Flicker in the Void

Tripping over my own two shoes,
Thought I'd conquered and paid my dues.
Reality's a joke in disguise,
Right when I think I've got it, surprise!

Birds chirping with gossip in the trees,
What do they know that brings me to my knees?
Sunshine flashes like a neon sign,
Wishing and hoping I can freely unwind.

Tea's too hot, yet I've sipped it all,
A single drop makes me jump and sprawl.
Laughter echoes in the clumsiness dance,
Living is funny, life's a wiggly trance.

The cat stares at me with knowing eyes,
"Why are you still here?" it seems to surprise.
Existence's antics, a whimsical game,
Filled with chuckles, never the same!

Embrace of the Unfamiliar

In the mirror, a stranger grins wide,
Is that really you or just a wild ride?
Shirt inside out, oh what a delight,
Fashion's new rules: 'It's wrong, but it's right.'

With a wiggle and jiggle, I hit the street,
People passing, each with a beat.
Are they laughing at me? Or with me, perhaps?
We're all in this circus; just check the maps!

A puzzling world that tumbles and spins,
Each new experience, a chance to begin.
Duck-faced selfies I can't quite understand,
Yet somewhere within, I'll take my stand.

Forever tripping on thoughts in my mind,
Searching for treasures so easy to find.
With a giggle, a snort, and wild disarray,
Let's toast to this dance, come what may!

Heartbeats in Stillness

Beating hearts in silent rooms,
Echo shadows, subduing glooms.
A lonely sock up on the floor,
I think it dreams of days of yore.

A chair creaks like a witty sage,
"Life's a play," it seems to gauge.
Dust bunnies waltz to a tune I can't hear,
Expressionless, yet alive, my dear!

Counting the cracks in the paint is a sport,
While doodling signs of life on a report.
Silly thoughts, like pop rocks that fizz,
Life's a blast, it turns with a whiz!

Even in stillness, laughter will bloom,
A cheeky ghost in my very own room.
So here's to existence, sweet and absurd,
Alive in the chaos, where joy is inferred!

An Unfurling Soul

Woke up today, tripped on my shoe,
Thought I was late, but what's new?
Coffee's a quest, it spills on my shirt,
Self-care routine? Time for dessert!

Mirror's reflection gives me a wink,
Who is that guy? Oh wait, it's pink!
Dance like a fish out of water, oh dear,
Laughing so hard, everyone can hear!

To-do lists float, they bubble and bounce,
Too many tasks, I start to renounce.
Yet here I am, with smiles to spare,
Giggling at life, breathing fresh air!

With snacks on my mind, I waddle and weave,
Life's just a ride, I giggle and leave.
An unfurling soul, in whimsical flight,
Finding my laugh in the slipstream of night.

Moments Caught in the Net of Time

Clock ticks loudly, my sandwich takes flight,
Chasing crumbs, oh what a sight!
Time is a net, and I'm just a fish,
Caught in the waves of my lunchtime wish.

Bumped into fate, she laughed with delight,
Said, 'What's your plan?' I replied, 'Not quite!'
Pants on backward or was it the shirt?
Fashion faux pas, but it didn't hurt!

Moments, they flicker like stars in a dream,
Why do they slip? Is it just my theme?
Spinning and swirling like leaves in the breeze,
Life's little folly, oh please, oh please!

Caught in a web, my thoughts all a-jumble,
Laughing with grace while I trip, then tumble.
Here's to the mishaps, the laughter, the rhyme,
In this quirky dance, I'm caught in the time.

Gazing into the Infinite

Staring at clouds, they're plotting a scheme,
One looks like pizza, or is that a dream?
I'm staring so hard, I enter a trance,
What if they're sent to offer me chance?

Gazing at stars, they sparkle and sing,
'Who are you?' they ask, 'Just a dust speckled thing!'
I wink back at them, they twinkle with glee,
As if they can tell I'm just plain crazy!

Infinity laughs; I snicker along,
In this cosmic dance, I'm part of the throng.
Caught in the moment, oh what a delight,
Finding my home in the depths of the night!

With each silly thought, I tickle the dark,
Gazing consumes me, ignites a spark.
What is existence but laughter and light?
Infinite giggles, oh, what a sight!

The Jolt of Here and Now

Boom! Here I am, what a sudden sound,
Reality hits me, feet on the ground.
Belly's a rumble, it's time to explore,
What's in the fridge? Oh, there's much more!

Socks on my hands, I'm ready for style,
Why should the floor be blank? Add a smile!
Each jolt of the day, a spark in my brain,
Dancing through chaos like I'm on a train.

Pants that won't fit, they giggle and moan,
Making new friends in the mirror, they groan.
'Laughter's a riddle,' the wise ones say,
I'm turning my life into a comedy play!

Here and now, life's juicy and ripe,
I toast to the flaws, raise a glass to the type.
With each silly foible, a wink and a grin,
The jolt's just begun; let the fun times begin!

Intrusions of Existence

Woke up today, my thoughts a mess,
Tripped on my shoelaces, what a stress.
Mirror said, 'Hey, who is this guy?'
Pants on backwards, I just can't lie.

Coffee's brewing, but I spill the cup,
Sipping slowly, then I look up.
Birds are chirping, a strange debate,
Why are they loud? It's already late!

Got lost in my socks, or is it just me?
Searching for answers, like fish in a tree.
Existence dances, a comical spree,
As I step out, I say, "What a day, whee!"

Life's a circus, a joyful ride,
With clowns and balloons always by my side.
Juggling worries, laughter's the prize,
Oh, the surprise of seeing with open eyes.

Stirring from a Dream

Fell from the clouds, with a thud and a grin,
Wondering how the day will begin.
Pajamas still on, in the light of dawn,
Chasing the cat, she's already gone!

Thought I could fly, till gravity called,
Turns out these dreams are just lightly walled.
Breakfast is waiting, but so is a mess,
Eggs in my hair? Oh, what a stress!

Found a sock monster, claimed he's my mate,
They probed for my shoes, said, "Don't tempt fate."
Laughter erupts, silly thoughts in the fray,
Who knew awareness could be this way?

Tangled in moments, I trip and I cheer,
Life's an odd puzzle; boy, it's unclear!
Yet all my misadventures, I hold them dear,
Every clumsy step, let's raise a cheer!

Fragments of a Waking Life

Sunshine breaks in, and I blink like a fool,
Staring at bread, confused by the rule.
But toast in my hand feels like gold,
Even if it's burnt, oh, the stories it told.

Trying to eat it, but crumbs fly around,
Squirrel outside gives me a curious sound.
Who knew breakfast could start a parade?
I'll dance with my toast, I'm feeling unmade!

Suddenly realized, my pet is a star,
Chasing her tail, she thinks it's bizarre.
Motion's contagious, I wobble and spin,
Laughing at life, oh, where to begin?

Stumbling through moments, collecting my glee,
Each pod of laughter is a key just for me.
Slice through the silence, let joy fill the air,
Dear fragments of waking, I'm ready to share!

The Weight of Awareness

Haunted by thoughts, I trip on the ground,
Awareness like bricks, heavy and round.
But oh, here's a squirrel, with a flash of a tail,
Life's quirky humor, it never seems stale.

Loading my plate with baked eggs and cheese,
Why do I feel like I'm lost in the breeze?
Juggling my worries, as birds start to sing,
The weight of a smile feels like a small thing.

Flip through the chaos, the jokes never end,
Each giggle a twist, as life seems to bend.
Laughter like bubbles, all popping around,
Chasing the confusion, freedom I've found!

Throwing my hands up, I dance to the grind,
Awareness a puzzle, with laughs intertwined.
So here's to the clumsies, the laughter, the cheer,
Embracing the crazy, let's kick up a gear!

Puzzles in the Pulse

I woke up today with a sock on my hand,
Wondering if my life was part of a band.
The toaster was humming a tune with pride,
And my coffee cup whispered, 'Enjoy the ride.'

My cat looked me over, as if in deep thought,
And I tried to recall where my marbles were caught.
Is this how the world spins, with bananas and dreams?
Or is reality woven with shimmering seams?

A puzzle of thoughts in this mind so bizarre,
Each piece clashing loudly like a random guitar.
But in every odd moment, I find a new jest,
Laughing through layers, I'm feeling quite blessed.

So here's to the chaos, the giggles, the quirks,
To the socks on my hands and the dance of the jerks.
For life's just a comedy, silly and sly,
Where laughter unravels, and we all learn to fly.

A Glimpse Beyond the Veil

I peered through the curtain where shadows do creep,
Spying on life while I'm snug in my sleep.
With whispers of nonsense, the universe played,
A melody of chaos, where logic had strayed.

The fridge light was glowing like stars in the night,
As I pondered existence and questioned my plight.
Do fish have a purpose beyond swimming in schools?
Or do they just flounder, breaking all the rules?

A puppet of fate, with strings I can't see,
Dancing through breakfast with glee and some glee.
The toast did a tango while I brewed my tea,
And I chuckled aloud, what is wrong with me?

A glimpse through the veil can be zany and bright,
When cereal critters band together in flight.
I may not have answers, but here's what is known,
In the theater of life, we're all just clones.

A Tapestry of Uncertainty

Woke up wrapped in uncertainty's weave,
Where socks lost their partners and time took its leave.
Bunny slippers bounced like they had dreams to chase,
While I searched for my car keys, lost in space.

The dog gave a bark like he was in on the joke,
As I stumbled around, trying not to croak.
Is the coffee a potion, or just burnt to a crisp?
Every day is a riddle, a whimsical lisp.

The walls had opinions, they whispered and sighed,
As I cracked all the eggs that my recipes lied.
Life's a grand buffet of delightful strange fare,
With a sprinkle of chaos, all served with a flare.

So here in this tapestry, loop after loop,
I'm tangled in laughter, in this vibrant group.
For who needs a map in this curious race?
When absurdity reigns and makes every place.

The Unseen Dance of Existence

In the kitchen, my blender did sway with delight,
While the dishes all gathered for a late-night fight.
The clock chimed a rhythm, like jazz for the brave,
But the rug just rolled over, not wanting to behave.

I pondered the purpose of ducks in a row,
Forgotten old biscuits that refuse to let go.
The plants on the windowsill plotted a coup,
While I tiptoed around in this peculiar zoo.

Existence, it turns out, is quite the odd jam,
Filled with hiccups and laughter, a life full of spam.
The universe chuckles, a cosmic report,
And I join in the dance, a delightful retort.

For in every hiccup and in each silly sway,
Life's an unseen dance that dares us to play.
So I'll twirl with the quirky and waltz with the wack,
Celebrating the moments that refuse to fall back.

Sudden Clarity in Chaos

In a crowd of bustling feet,
I trip on my own shoelace.
A moment's pause, my heart skips,
Life's a comedy, a wild race.

Coffee spills upon my shirt,
I laugh at my morning mess.
In chaos, I find the quirks,
Odd rhythms, life's own dress.

Beneath the chaos of the day,
I hear a pigeon coo its song.
A simple tune amidst the fray,
Reminds me, I do belong.

In moments lost to time and space,
I chuckle at the grand design.
Caught in jokes, a silly face,
Alive, I sip this life like wine.

Waking Up to Paradoxes

Alarm clocks ring with vigor loud,
I snooze and dream of chocolate cake.
Waking up, I'm still a kid,
In this grown-up, noisy wake.

I wear my socks that don't quite match,
Fashion rules? They can take a hike.
With toast burnt black, I make my pitch,
Trying to fit, yet go on strike.

In simple truths, I find the jest,
With every wrong turn, humor grows.
Life's a puzzle, I confess,
Playful twists and silly prose.

As the day flips, I laugh once more,
Dancing through life's heavy script.
Finding joy in each uproar,
I'm a comedian, on a trip.

When Stillness Speaks

In silence thick, a thought arrives,
My brain's a circus, spinning fast.
A golden moment filled with wise,
'Alive' is the joke that lasts.

The cat is napping, dreams in tow,
While I'm deciphering life's big play.
A rock's stillness, yet it grows,
In every quiet, mischief lay.

With every breath, the world unwinds,
In simplest things, I find my glee.
A leaf that falls, a whimsy binds,
Life's playful quirk is plain to see.

From stillness comes the loudest cheer,
In mundane truths, the laughter hides.
Alive in chaos, it's all so clear,
In every breath, humor resides.

Glimpses of Existence

A raindrop dances on my nose,
I laugh at nature's dripping art.
Each splash is poetry that flows,
A symphony, a world apart.

The toaster pops, and bread takes flight,
I greet the morning with a grin.
Each moment shines, just feels so right,
In every mishap, fun begins.

A fly buzzes, it makes me squeal,
Yet in its chaos, joy's quite clear.
Life's whimsy is the perfect meal,
A buffet of laughs we hold dear.

With every glance, we twist and spin,
In life's great play, there's no regret.
The humor found in where we've been,
Alive is the best joke, I bet.

Moments of Serene Unease

I tripped on my shoelace, oh what a sight,
A dance of my feet in the fading light.
I laughed at the fall, though my pride took a hit,
Life's comic relief, and I can't seem to quit.

A sneeze in a meeting, the silence was loud,
Everyone turned, like I drew a crowd.
I chuckled and waved, so what if I blew,
Being human's a joy, with a dash of the blue.

Mismatched socks in a world full of gray,
Waking up late, oh it's just another day.
Coffee stains on my shirt, a dapper cliché,
But hey, it's my style—who's got time to play?

As I stumble through life with a grin on my face,
Embracing the chaos, my own little race.
Glimmers of laughter in spots that surprise,
Awake in the moment, I'm done with the lies.

Beneath the Surface of Routine

Alarm rings at dawn, I groan and I yawn,
Coffee in hand, I shuffle, move on.
Shoes on the wrong feet, I laugh as I trip,
Life's a grand circus, a non-stop comic strip.

Hours blur by, like marshmallows in stew,
Chasing my thoughts, like a cat chasing dew.
Meetings and emails, they stretch and they sprawl,
Yet here in the chaos, I'm having a ball.

My sock drawer's a puzzle, a colorful mess,
Matching with mismatches, I guess it's no stress.
Lunch at my desk, a sandwich on the run,
But this silly dance is, oh, so much fun!

Every tiny blunder, I take with a grin,
Adventures in boredom, my life's little win.
Routine's just a canvas, and I'm the delight,
Painting my days in laughter, not fright.

In the Garden of Now

Sunshine tickles my face, I squint and I grin,
Weeds are my rivals, let the games begin!
A butterfly flutters, like it's lost its way,
Nature's a party, come join in the play.

The roses are blushing, the daisies all peek,
In this garden of now, every moment's unique.
I trip over roots, and giggle with glee,
Life's such a garden, come wander with me.

Squirrels in tuxedos, they dance on the grass,
Chasing their tails, giggling as they pass.
Dandelion wishes, they scatter and play,
I toss mine up too, come what may, come what may!

With dirt on my hands and a smile on my face,
Life's just a flower, a curious race.
Each petal like laughter, each moment I sow,
In the garden of now, there's magic to grow.

Chasing Elusive Whys

Why does my toaster have a dance of its own?
Burnt toast in the morning, my breakfast is blown.
The cat gives me judgment, she thinks I'm derailed,
Chasing my questions, like a ship with no sail.

Why does the moon glow with such silver delight?
It winks through my window, a mischievous sight.
I ponder the cosmos while wearing my socks,
Life's a puzzling riddle, it unravels and rocks.

Why do we giggle at things so absurd?
Like slipping on ice, or tripping on words?
In the tilt of my world, I find joy in the mess,
Each question a riddle, an eternal caress.

So I'll keep on asking, with glee and with cheer,
Life's wild amusement, it's perfectly clear.
In the quest for the answers, I'll dance and I'll sigh,
With laughter as my compass, I'll reach for the sky.

The Unfolding of Me

A morning routine like a poorly-scripted play,
One sock on my foot, the other astray.
Mirror reflects a face, it winks back with glee,
In the unfolding chapters, I'm still getting free.

Who knew my lunch bag could hold such delights?
A snack and a sandwich, oh, what a sight!
Carrot sticks hiding, like secrets to keep,
My life's like a puzzle, layers too deep.

Chasing ambition, like jelly on toast,
Spreading it thick, but I'm still a funny host.
Each day a new page, each laugh a confetti,
In this big book of life, nothing's quite steady.

So I'll scribble my story in colors so bright,
With every misstep, I'll twirl into the light.
The unfolding of me is a whimsical spree,
Like a kite in the wind, I'll just let it be.

www.ingramcontent.com/pod-product-compliance
Lightning Source LLC
Chambersburg PA
CBHW071837160426
43209CB00003B/326